DOODLE

WHILE YOU WORK

ABOUT THE ARTIST:

Staffan Gnosspelius is an artist, illustrator and print maker.
Originally from Lund in Sweden, he is now based in London.
He has written and illustrated a number of books for children and
adults, including *Gå och bada Mister Räf!* and *Over the Himalayas*.

For more information and examples of his work, please visit
www.gnosspelius.com.

DOODLE
WHILE YOU WORK

STAFFAN GNOSSPELIUS

MICHAEL O'MARA BOOKS

First published in Great Britain in 2008 by
Michael O'Mara Books Limited
9 Lion Yard
Tremadoc Road
London SW4 7NQ

A CIP catalogue record for this book is available from the British Library

Papers used by Michael O'Mara Books Limited are natural, recyclable
products made from wood grown in sustainable forests. The manufacturing
processes conform to the environmental regulations of the country of origin.

ISBN: 978-1-84317-294-9

10 9 8 7 6 5 4 3 2 1

Design by Design 23

Printed and bound in Great Britain by William Clowes Ltd, Beccles, Suffolk

www.mombooks.com

INTRODUCTION

Many of us find ourselves doodling at some point during the working day, whether it's while we're put 'on hold' yet again, during a particularly dull meeting, or when we're feeling the urge to express creatively just what we'd like to do to Mr Mean from Accounts . . . Whether in moments of sheer boredom, or high imagination, *Doodle While You Work* is your ideal companion.

But many of us find we're often stuck for inspiration. Never fear – *Doodle While You Work* contains over 200 incomplete or barely started doodles for you to develop and finish in any way you wish. The humorous, wildly imaginative captions that accompany each doodle offer hints to guide your pen or pencil, but the outcome is entirely up to you. Now is the time to dream up new office artwork, plan your escape route, plot your revenge and redefine the inner workings of the coffee machine, while some feathery but flightless friends make regular appearances along the way. To work! – put down that blueberry muffin/annual financial report/gun, pick up your pen and get doodling! Amazing things can happen when you *Doodle While You Work* . . .

Draw the estimated number of cups of tea consumed in your office today.

Design the new reception area and receptionist.

What lives in the toilet?

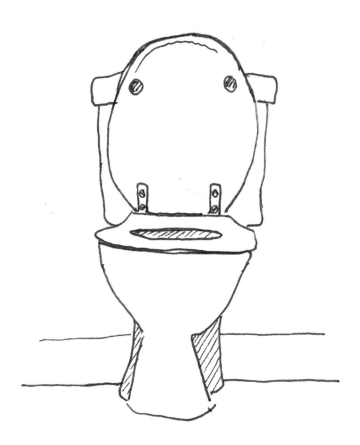

Complete the design for the new staffroom wallpaper.

Where does the door at the end of the corridor lead and what lurks there?

Complete the new office layout

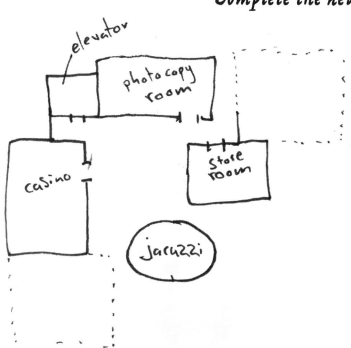

Create a new abstract painting for the boardroom.

Complete the cupcake mountain scoffed by you and your workmates each week.

Fill in the happy/disappointed faces when the pay rises come through.

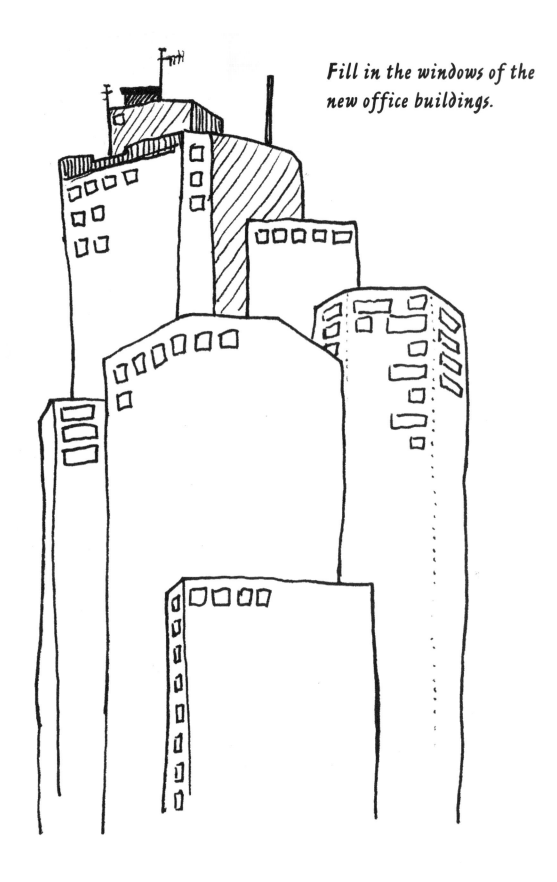

Fill in the windows of the new office buildings.

Fill the elevator with penguins.

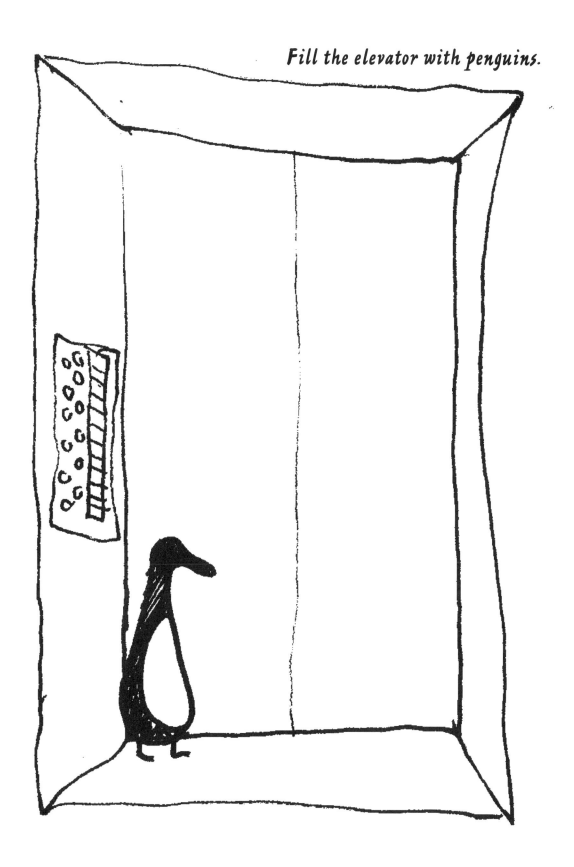

What's about to be flattened?

What's falling from the shelf?

. . . *and his secretary.*

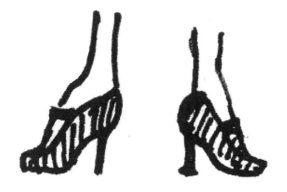

Draw the rest of the dirty mug mountain at the end of the day.

Who got stuck in the fence?

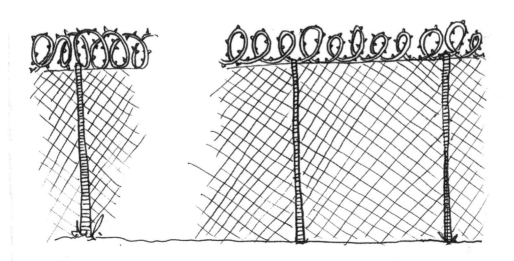

Add flowers to the bouquet
for the boss's wife.

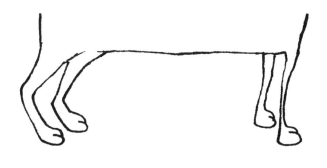

Draw the invisible computer-crashing animal that roams the office from time to time.

Fill in the faces sitting opposite you on the way to work.

What would you lob at the courier if you knew you could get away with it?

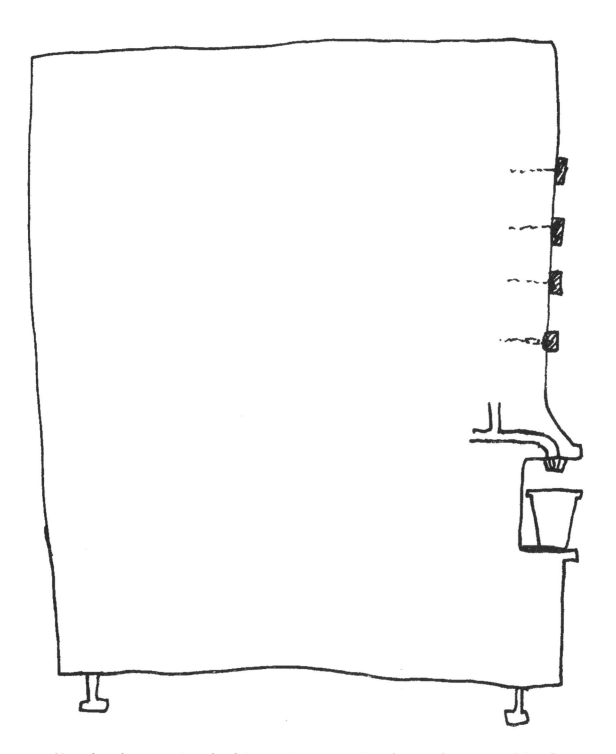

How do they make the disgusting soup in the vending machine?

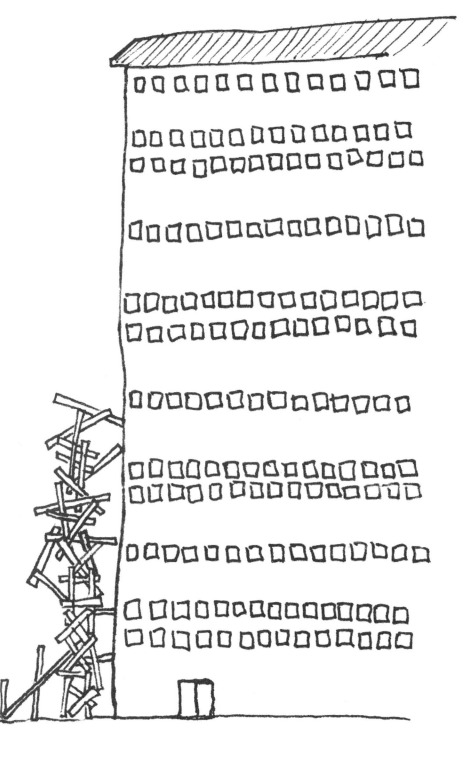

Complete the scaffolding on the side of the factory.

What's inside the leaving-do cake for...........................?

*What are the penguins hiding
from the Supervisor?*

*What is the Supervisor
hiding from the
penguins?*

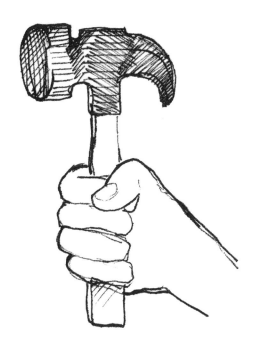

What is the variable-adjustment tool amending?

Work entrance 9 a.m.

Work entrance 5 p.m.

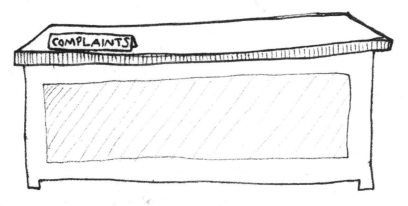

Who or what would you have dealing with complaints?

What kidnapped the computer technician?

What's taking up three spaces in the car park?

Show the
poltergeist that
tangles the
phone wire.

How many more penguins are smoking outside?

What did the window cleaner see in the storeroom?

Who is always first in line for the sandwich trolley?

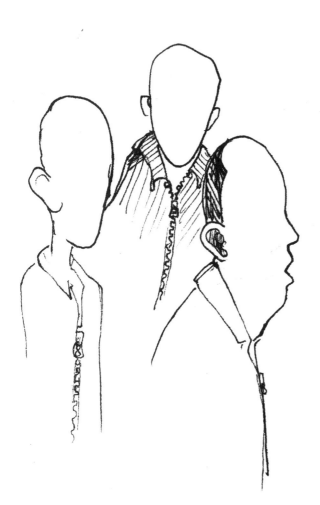 

Show what happens when she crosses the factory floor.

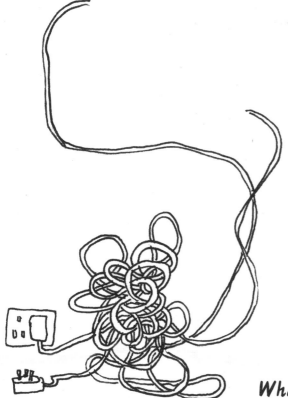

What is plugged in and what's not?

What is this worker dreaming about?

What can you see out of your window?

What are the penguins looking at?

Finish off the doodle of the night guard.

Complete the drinks table after the Christmas party.

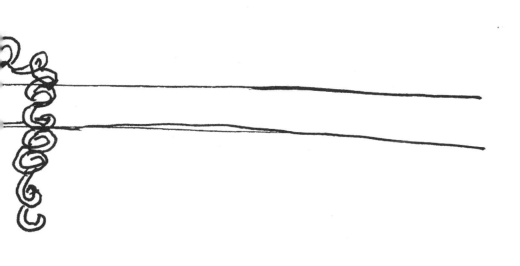

Pile your workload on this unfortunate snail.

Monday   **Tuesday**   **Wednesday**   **Thursday**

Design different tie patterns for the whole week.

Friday

What's going on in the cleaner's cupboard?

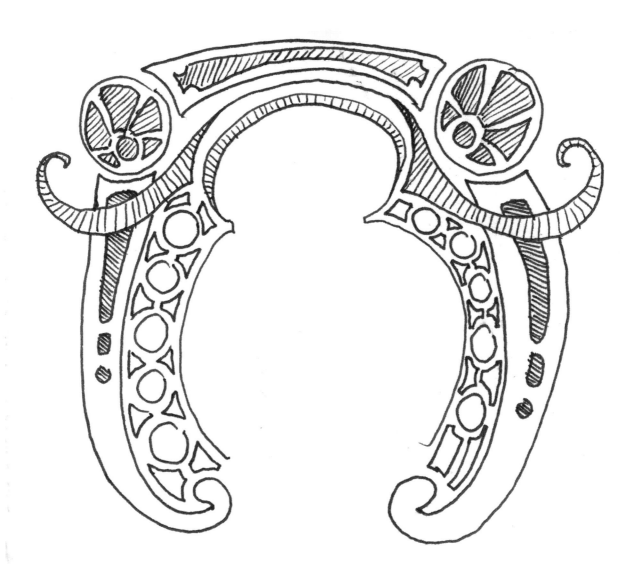

Who at work is an angel in disguise?

Show the warehouse manager's different styles of comb-over hair.

What is hiding in the filing cabinets?

How many hands and tools does an overworked employee need?

What's being used to sign the contract?

What kind of getaway car would you have to escape from work?

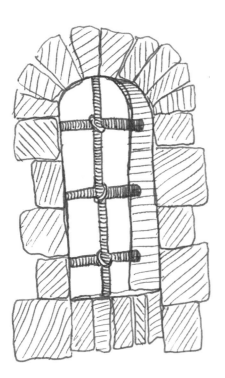

Who or what should be
kept in a dark tower far,
far away?

What's being transported by the penguin?

Complete the design for the new reception wallpaper.

What's causing the rush hour traffic jam?

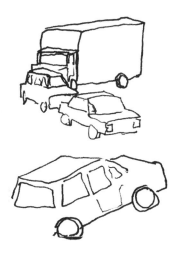

Can the sleeping security guard's snores
tell you what he's dreaming about?

Complete the pile of money that you would like to be paid today.

Finish the queue of paperclips waiting to use the photocopier.

Fill the jars with biscuits, nail clippings and other random stuff.

useful   *pointless*   *personal*   *plain annoying*

Estimate your email/memo piles after a full working day.

Design the new plant display to brighten the environment by the photocopier.

Continue the plant display into the reception area.

Extend the display with carnivorous plants into the boss's office.

Design your new office chair.

What is the most valuable object in your boss's office?

Complete the number of bottles to be recycled after the boss's Friday 'working lunch'.

Fill in the smile on pay day.

How many new penguins are being welcomed to the company?

How many paperclips are queuing to use the ladies' loo?

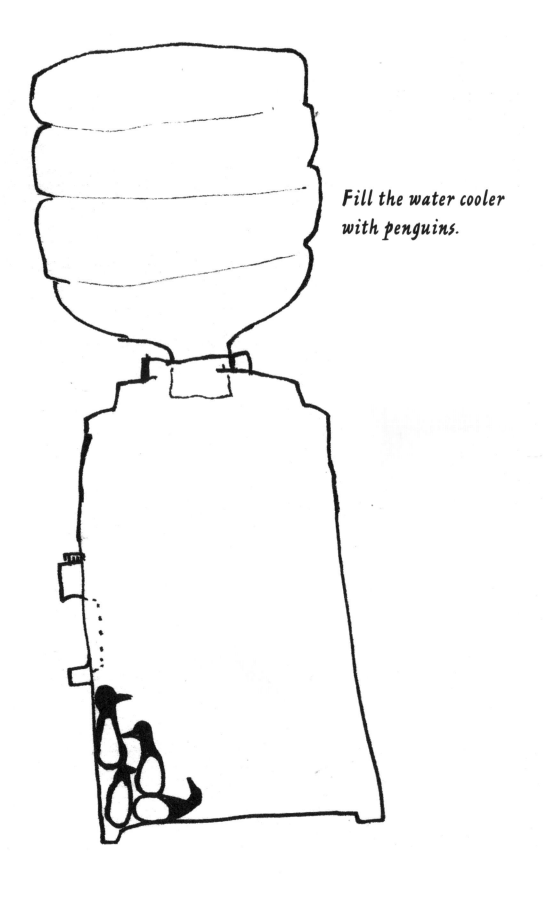

Fill the water cooler
with penguins.

Draw the rest of the paper-eating snake
that causes the printer to jam.

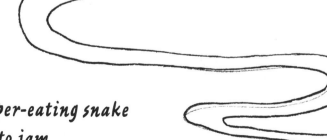

What lives under the table in the boardroom?

Complete the correction-fluid plant.

Draw the rest of the paperclips who are out on strike.

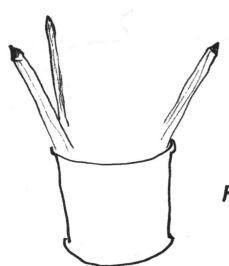

Fill the jar with failing ballpoint pens.

What graffiti would you scrawl
in the toilet if you knew you
could get away with it?

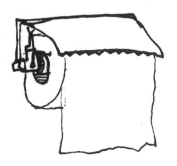

Fill the page with bananas that have been thrown out by someone who thinks they smell too much of banana.

How many more penguins are waiting for the bus?

Fill the boss's sausage dog with sausages and other assorted stuff he's eaten.

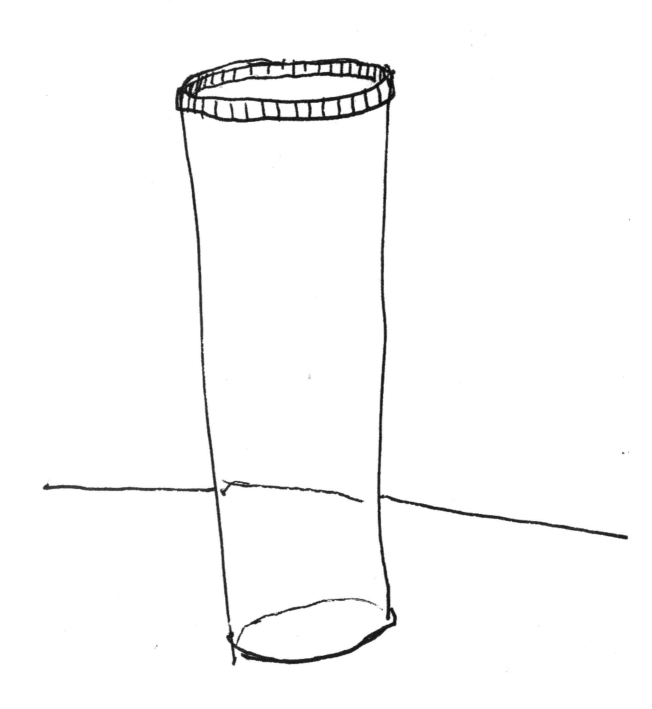

What would you put in the boss's drink?

Fill the coffee machine with cog wheels.

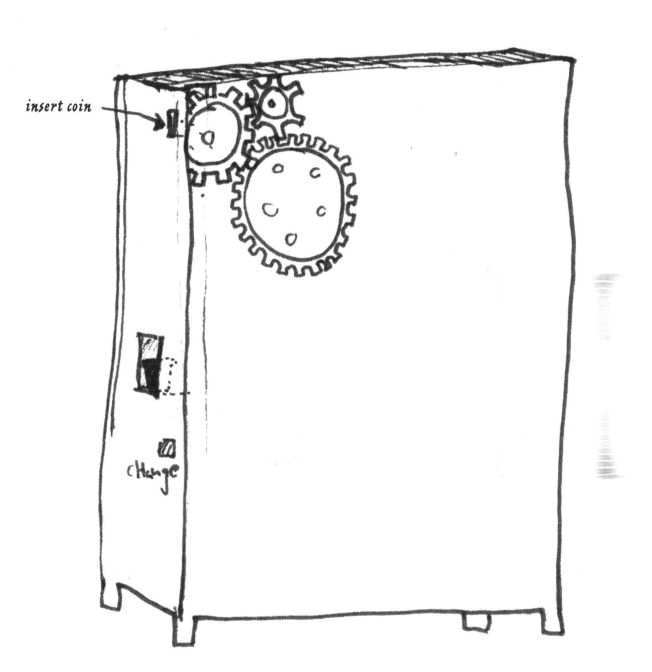

insert coin

change

Draw the body count of mangled paperclips after the regular Monday meeting.

Estimate the general mood in your workplace with proportions of:

♡ happiness   ✰ effectiveness    stress

What animal should never be allowed in the elevator?

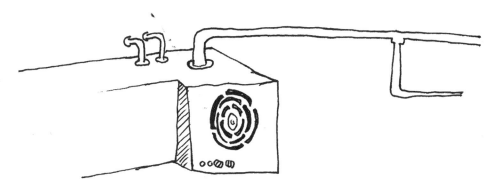

What makes the noise inside the radiator?

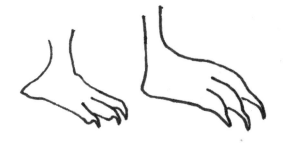

Show what the 'IN-tray Monster'
looks like.

And his brother.

How many penguins does it take to change the fluorescent lighting?

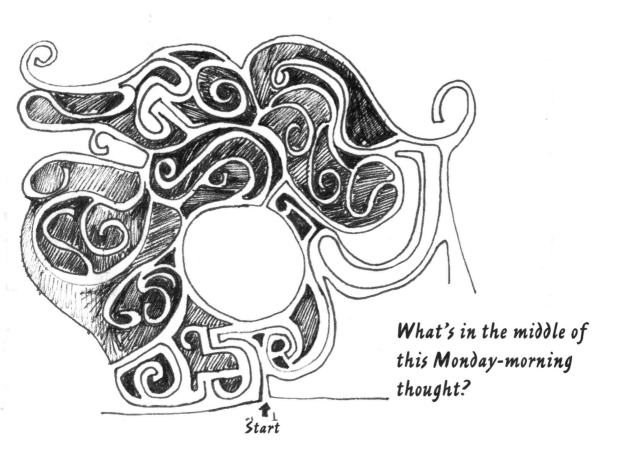

What's in the middle of this Monday-morning thought?

Start

Draw the Sudoku-eating creature.

What comes out if you open the valve?

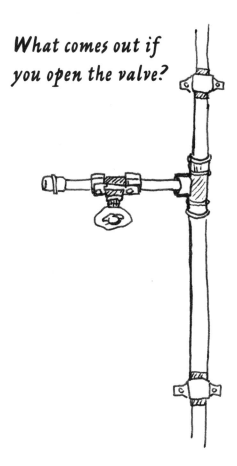

Fill in the pollution and its effects.

How many more cogs and wheels start turning
when the light is switched on?

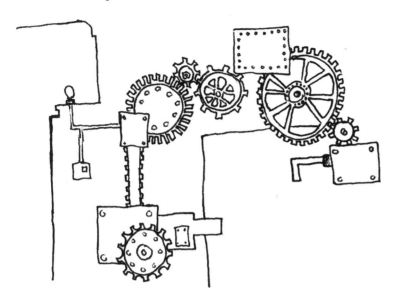

What was he not expecting to be <u>packing</u> and stacking today?

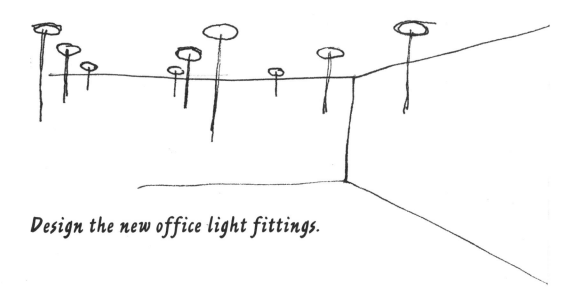

Design the new office light fittings.

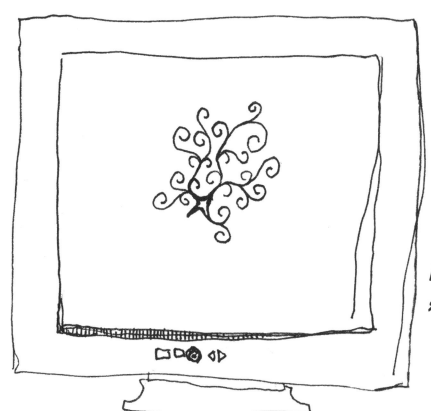

Design your new screen saver.

What's stuck in the zip?

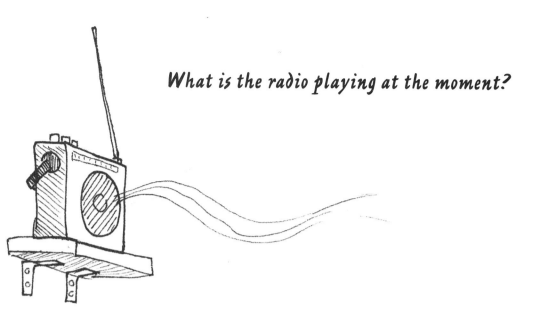

What is the radio playing at the moment?

What treasure might you find
at the bottom of your 'IN' tray?

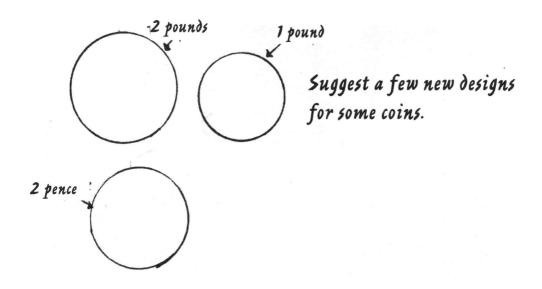

2 pounds

1 pound

2 pence

Suggest a few new designs
for some coins.

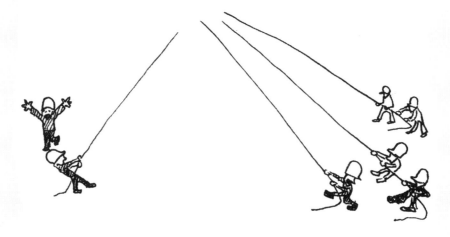

What has been captured in the warehouse?

Who or what needs to be cooled down?

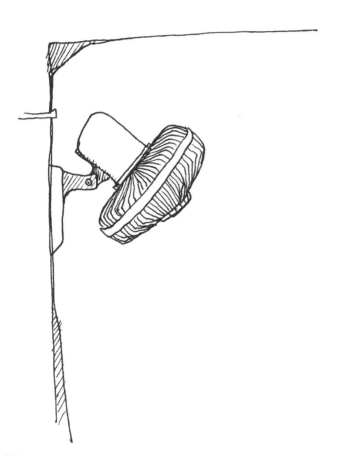

Complete the yawn at the end of the day.

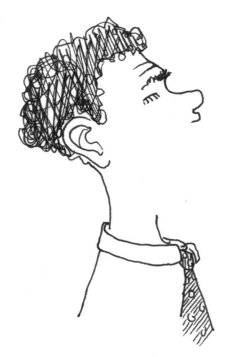

Complete the yawn at the end of the week.

Complete the yawn at the end of the month . . .

. . . and at the end of the financial year.

How many penguins are still on the bus?

What's the first thing you would throw out of the window in an emergency?

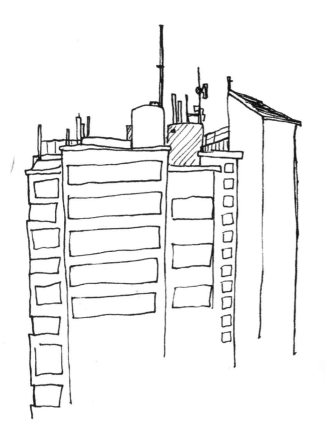

Draw the flag on top
of the office.

Fill the page with smiley faces and one miserable secretary face.

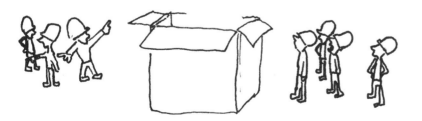

What did no one expect
to be in this delivery?

What happened to
the three warehouse
shelf stackers?

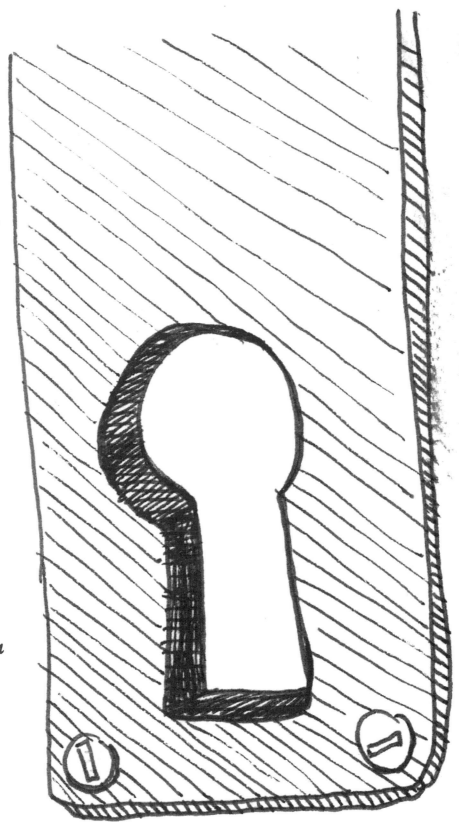

What's
happening in
the boss's
office?

Draw the ghost who feeds on your soul each time you have lunch at your desk.

Who won the first prize for fancy dress?

What do the new tiles in the
toilets look like?

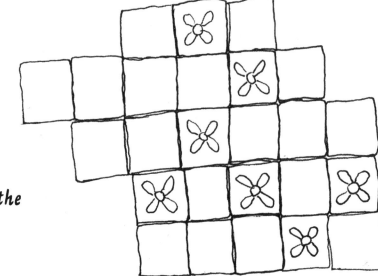

What's under surveillance in the car park?

Complete the
paperclip battle.

Draw your favourite lunch.

Complete the pile the postman is delivering.

Complete the pile the postman is delivering at Christmas.

*Complete the pile the
postman is delivering to you
on Valentine's Day.*

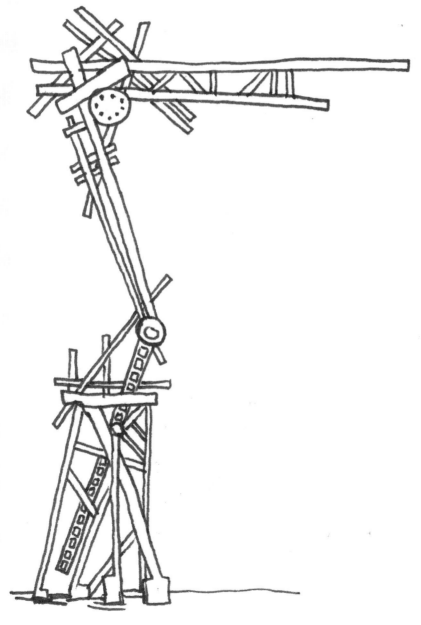

What is this scaffolding holding up?

Complete the sugar-cube pyramid.

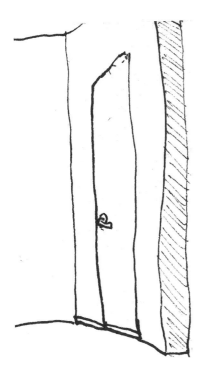

What lives in the store cupboard?

How many penguins are escaping from work by balloon?

Show more flames and exploding parts on the photocopier that is out of order yet again.

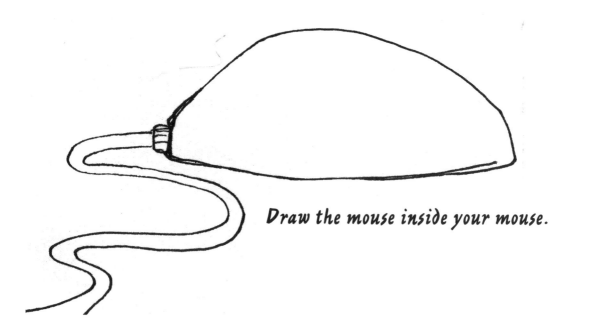

Draw the mouse inside your mouse.

How many teeth are in the sales rep's smile?

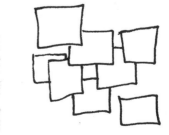

Fill the page with the never-ending supply of annoying Post-it notes.

What's the best Christmas bonus you could get from Santa?

Where are the penguins?

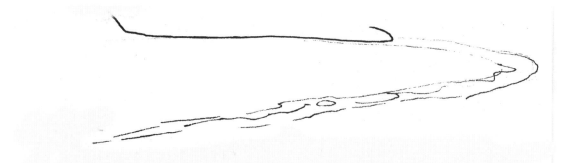

Draw the time slug that slows down time at the end of Tuesday afternoons.

Complete the food chain.

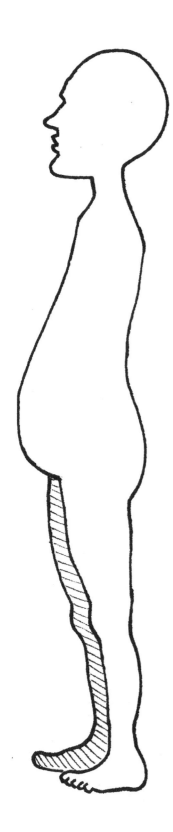

Show the trapped and non-trapped wind.

Complete the paperclips'
Christmas party.

What happens to the pigeon on the window ledge?

What do you do when the
photocopier goes mental?

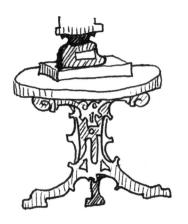

Design the bust to be placed in the entrance hall.

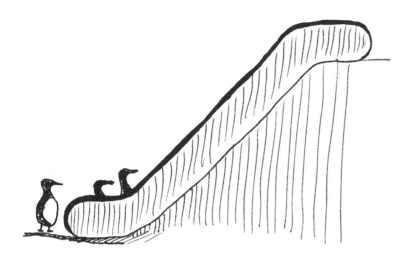

How many penguins are using the escalator?

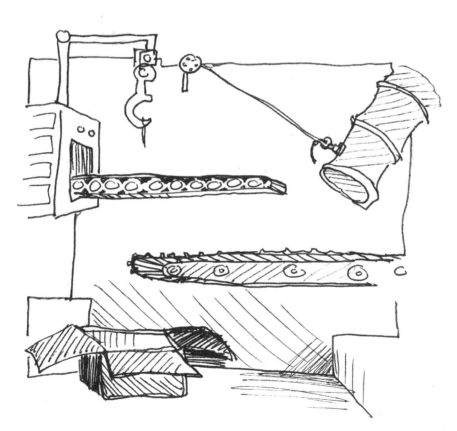

What's being produced today?

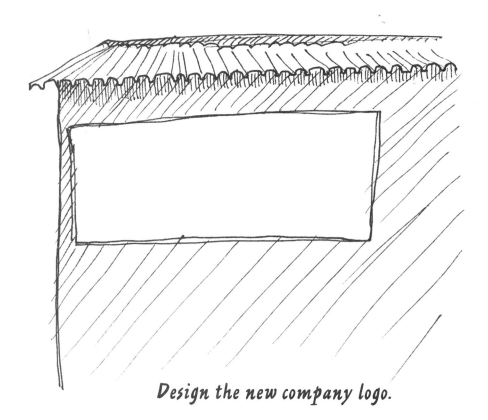

Design the new company logo.

Fill the toothpaste tube with paracetamol.

What could you cook over the fire made with correspondence from the accounts department?

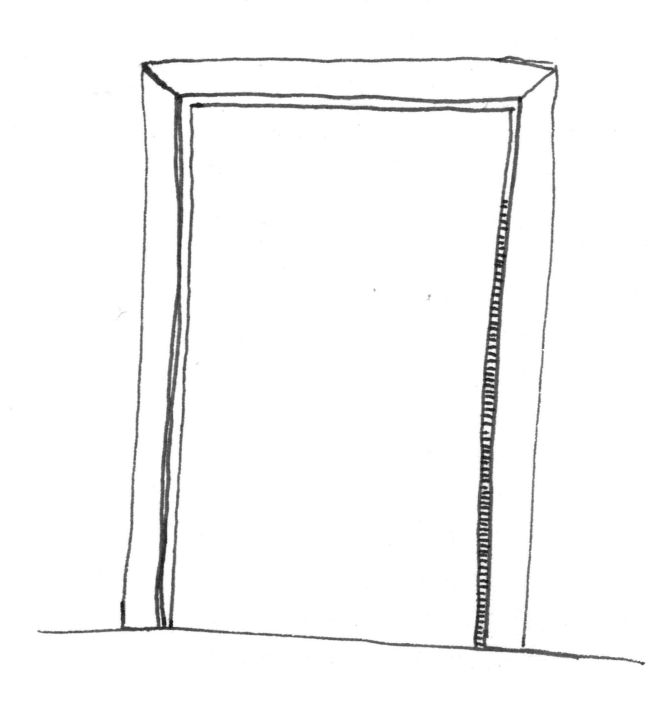

How many padlocks and bolts are on the stationery cupboard door?

How many penguins live in the fire extinguisher?

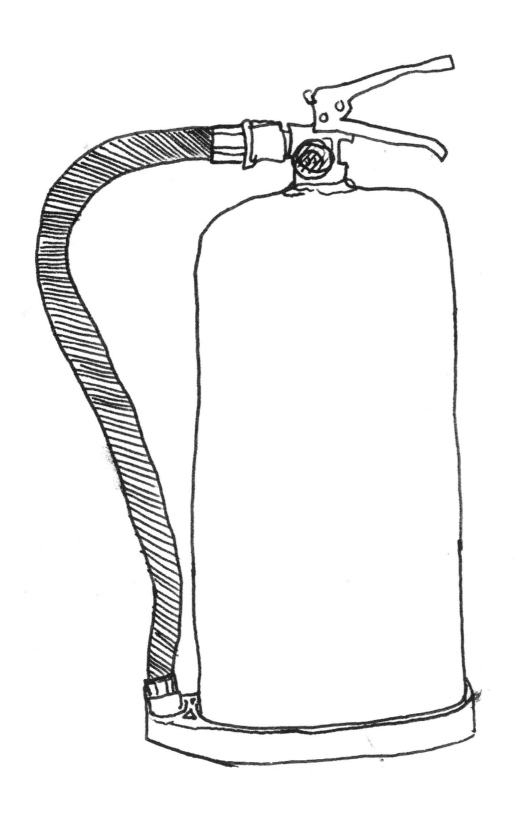

Fill in the buttons on the control console and show what they are controlling.

What does the new cleaner look like?

What's causing the funny smell in the boardroom?

*The boss is
actually a . . .*

→

top **Secret** file

name:. . . . .
alias:. . . . . . .
reality:. . . . .

Why shouldn't you take the turn-off?

How many penguins are escaping from work and how many are staying?

Draw the new guard dog.

Design different earrings to be worn this week.

Monday

Tuesday

Wednesday

Thursday

Friday

Fill in the boss's reaction.

Show what happens at
the leaving-do.

Who's throwing the stapler at whom?

What's at the top of the invoice pile?

What lives in the factory gatehouse?

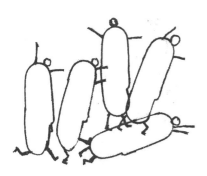

Complete the paperclip stampede heading for the canteen.

How many more *penguins* are about to be flattened by the reversing van?

Complete the piles of magazines in the staff room.

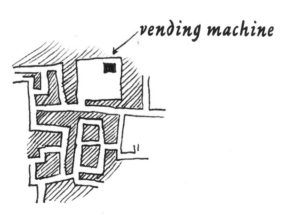

vending machine

Complete the maze to find the
vending machine in the basement.

Who's drinking the extra large, extra strong latte with an extra shot?

Fill in the hierarchical pyramid for your workplace.

Show the rest of the penguins waiting for a train.

How you feel.

How you should be feeling.

How you will be feeling on Friday afternoon.

What's held up by the weights?

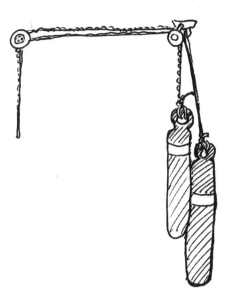

What's stuck?

Complete the design for the new boardroom wallpaper.

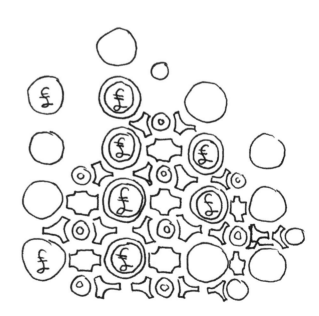

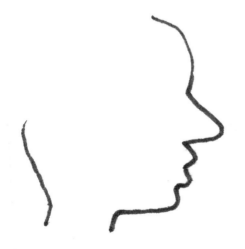

Complete the hairdos.

Show Mr Nice who's giving the penguins a lift to work.

Complete the body behind
the sexy voice you hear when
you order more paperclips.